*Indian Pigeons and Doves In Color*
*An Art Book of Wild Doves and Pigeons from India*


*by E.C. Stuart Baker*

**with an introduction by Jackson Chambers**


*This work contains material that was originally published in 18913.*

*This publication is within the Public Domain.*

*This edition is reprinted for educational purposes
and in accordance with all applicable Federal Laws.*

*Introduction Copyright 2018 by Jackson Chambers*

# The World's Largest Selection of Vintage Poultry Books

# www.VintagePoultry.com

# Self Reliance Books

Get more historic titles on animal and stock breeding, gardening and old fashioned skills by visiting us at:

http://selfreliancebooks.blogspot.com/

# *Introduction*

I am pleased to present yet another historic title on raising Pigeons.


The work is in the Public Domain and is re-printed here in accordance with Federal Laws.

As with all reprinted books of this age that are intended to perfectly reproduce the original edition, considerable pains and effort had to be undertaken to correct fading and sometimes outright damage to existing proofs of this title. At times, this task is quite monumental, requiring an almost total "rebuilding" of some pages from digital proofs of multiple copies. Despite this, imperfections still sometimes exist in the final proof and may detract from the visual appearance of the text. The original plates in these titles are often moved to the rear of the text to adhere to modern publication standards.

I hope you enjoy reading this book as much as I enjoyed making it available to readers again.


Jackson Chambers

THE ASHY-HEADED GREEN PIGEON—*OSMOTRERON P. PHAYREI*
(½ Nat. Size—Male on right, female on left.)

THE BURMESE GREEN PIGEON—*CROCOPUS (PH. VIRIDIFRONS.*

(½ Nat. Size.)

THE CINNAMON-HEADED GREEN PIGEON—*OSMOTRERON FULVICOLLIS.*
(½ Nat. Size—Male on left, female on right.)

PLATE 2

THE LESSER ORANGE-BREASTED GREEN PIGEON—*OSMOTRERON B. BICINCTA.*

($\frac{1}{2}$ Nat. Size—Male on left, female on right.)      PLATE 3

THE LARGE THICK-BILLED GREEN PIGEON—*BUTRERON CAPELLII.*

($\frac{1}{2}$ Nat. Size—Male below, female above.)          PLATE 4

THE THICK-BILLED GREEN PIGEON—*TRERON NIPALENSIS.*

(½ Nat. Size— Male on right, female on left.)

THE PIN-TAILED GREEN PIGEON—*SPHENOCERCUS APICAUDA.*

($\frac{1}{2}$ Nat. Size—Male on left, female on right.)

PLATE 6

THE GREEN IMPERIAL PIGEON—*CARPOPHAGA O. OENEA.*

(⅓ Nat. Size.)

PLATE 7

THE GREY-HEADED IMPERIAL PIGEON—*DUCULA INSIGNIS GRISEICAPILLA.*

(½ Nat. Size.)

PLATE 8

**THE PIED IMPERIAL PIGEON—*MYRISTICIVORA BICOLOR*.**

(½ Nat. Size.)

PLATE 9

THE NICOBAR PIGEON—*CALAENAS NICOBARICA.*

(½ Nat. Size.)

PLATE 10

THE BRONZE-WINGED DOVE—*CHALCOPHAPS INDICA.*

(½ Nat. Size—Male on left, female on right.)

BLUE HILL-PIGEON—*COLUMBA RUPESTRIS.*

(⅓ Nat. Size.)

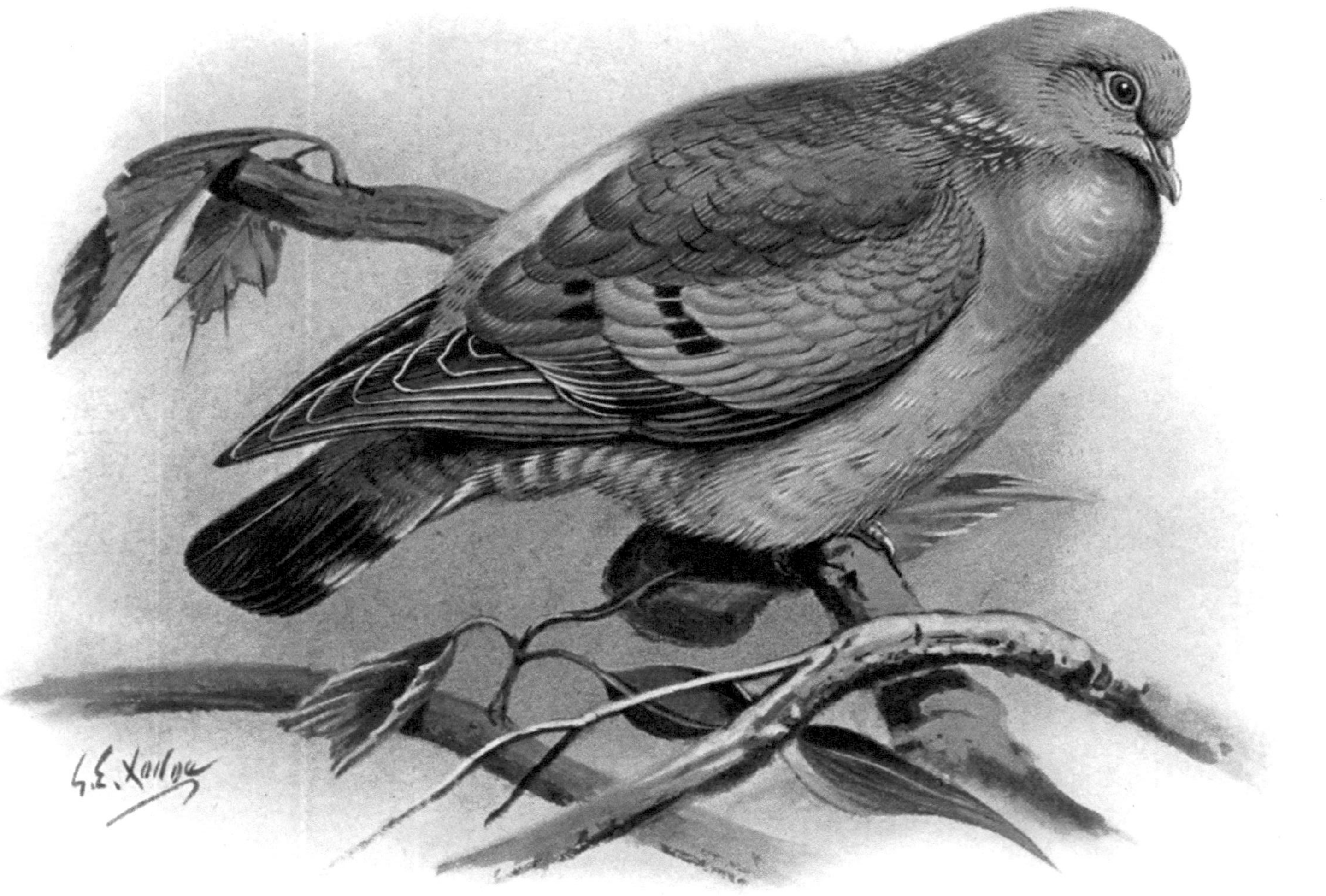

THE EASTERN STOCK-PIGEON—*COLUMBA OENAS EVERSMANNI.*

($\frac{1}{2}$ Nat. Size.)

THE SNOW-PIGEON—*COLUMBA LEUCONOTA.*

($\frac{1}{2}$ Nat. Size.)

PLATE 14

THE SPECKLED WOOD-PIGEON—*DENDROTRERON HODGSONI.*
($\frac{1}{2}$ Nat Size—Male above, female below.)

PLATE 15

THE EASTERN WOOD-PIGEON OR RING-DOVE—*PALUMBUS P. CASIOTIS.*

(⅔ Nat. Size.)

PLATE 16

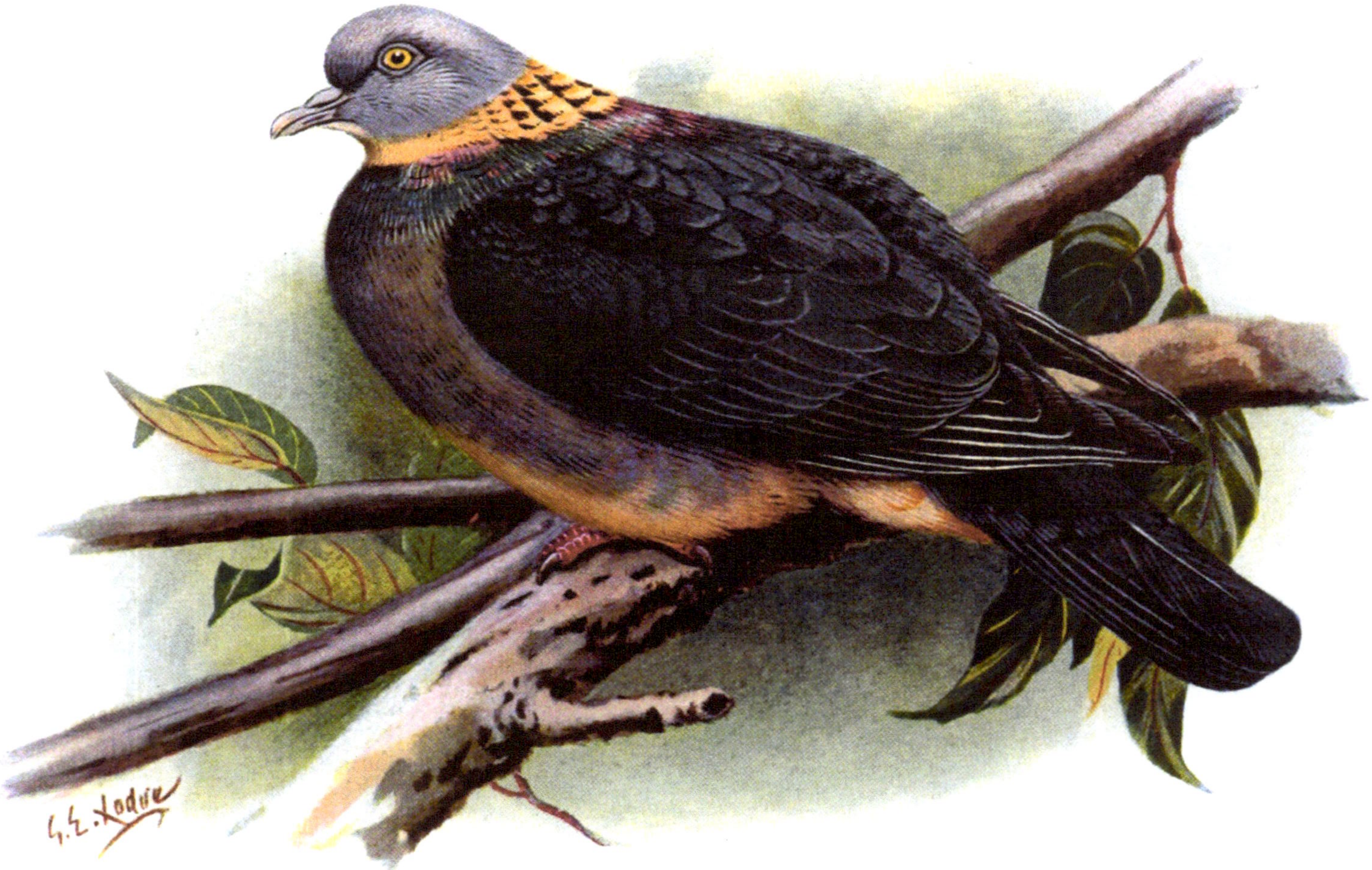

THE ASHY WOOD-PIGEON—*ALSOCOMUS PULCHRICOLLIS.*

(⅓ Nat. Size.)

THE PURPLE WOOD-PIGEON—*ALSOCOMUS PUNICEUS*
(⅓ Nat. Size—Male above, female below.)     PLATE 18

THE ANDAMANESE WOOD-PIGEON—*ALSOCOMUS PALUMBOIDES*.

(½ Nat. Size.)

PLATE 19

SYKES'S TURTLE-DOVE—*STREPTOPELIA T. MEENA.*

($\frac{1}{2}$ Nat. Size.)

PLATE 20

THE MALAY SPOTTED DOVE—*STREPTOPELIA S. TIGRINA.*

(½ Nat. Size.)

PLATE 21

THE LITTLE BROWN DOVE—*STREPTOPELIA CAMBAYENSIS.*

(½ Nat. Size—Male on left, female on right.)

PLATE 22

**THE BURMESE RED TURTLE-DOVE—*OENOPOPELIA T. HUMILIS.***

(½ Nat. Size—Male on left, female on right.)        PLATE 23

THE BAR-TAILED CUCKOO-DOVE—*MACROPYGIA TUSALIA*

(½ Nat. Size—Male on right, female on left.)

PLATE 24

THE ANDAMAN CUCKOO-DOVE—*MACROPYGIA RUFIPENNIS.*
(½ Nat Size—Male on right, female on left.)
PLATE 25

THE BARRED GROUND-DOVE—*GEOPELIA STRIATA*.

(½ Nat. Size—Male on left, juvenile on right.)

PLATE 26

www.ingramcontent.com/pod-product-compliance
Lightning Source LLC
Chambersburg PA
CBHW040203240726
48664CB00002B/813